102 Animal Jokes

by Ski Michaels

Watermill Press

Library of Congress Cataloging-in-Publication Data

Michaels, Ski.
   102 animal jokes / by Ski Michaels, author & illustrator.
      p.   cm.
   Summary: A collection of animal jokes, including "Why didn't
the elephant get rich? He was willing to work for peanuts."
   ISBN 0-8167-2613-2 (pbk.)
   1. Wit and humor, Juvenile.   2. Animals—Juvenile humor.
[1. Jokes.   2. Riddles.   3. Animals—Wit and humor.]   I. Title.
PN6163.M5   1992
818'.5402—dc20   91-30061

Printed in the United States of America.

10   9   8   7   6   5   4   3   2   1

Why was the duck unhappy?

His bill was in the mail.

Why didn't the dog speak to his foot?

It's not polite to talk back to your paw.

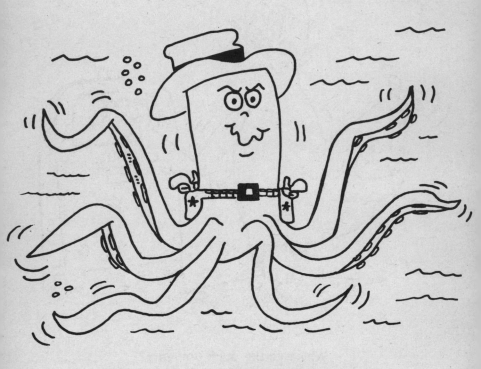

**Which undersea creature has lots of arms
and is fast on the draw?**

Billy the Squid.

How much money do a dozen skunks have?

Twelve scents (cents).

What's the quickest way to mail a little horse?

Use the Pony Express.

Why did Mr. and Mrs. Cat get married?

They were a purr-fect match.

How do turtles pay for things?

They shell out cash.

How did the mouse pass his final exam?

He just squeaked by.

Why was the little elephant six hours late for dinner?

He had to wash behind his ears before coming to the table.

Which birds work underground?

Myna (miner) birds.

Which bird does construction work?

The crane.

Why was the lion all wet?

He had a water-mane (water-main) break.

What's gray and spins around and around?

A hippo stuck in a revolving door.

Why did the pigeon need to get out?

He was cooped up at home all week.

What did the mole publisher print?

An underground newspaper.

Why do fish like to eat worms so much?

Who knows? They're just hooked on them.

When did the steers go west?

During the Cow-a-fornia Gold Rush.

What did the baby horse say to the barn?

Is my fodder (father) in there?

Why was the pig mad at the hog?

The hog squealed on him.

What do you call mail sent to a cat?

Kitty letter.

**What loves peanuts and goes boom!
boom! boom?**

An elephant skipping rope.

What kind of ducks rob banks?

Safe quackers.

Why was the fox so depressed?

Everyone kept hounding him.

What did one pig cowboy say to the other?

Reach for the sty, partner.

What do you call a Georgia hen who changes the color of her feathers?

Southern dyed chicken.

What did the gander wear to his wedding?

A *duck*cedo (tuxedo).

Why was the elephant annoyed at his date?

She took too long to powder her nose.

How do you send a canary through the post office?

Use bird-class (first-class) mail.

What do you call a formal dance for ducks?

A fowl ball.

What did the little chick say to the big chick?

Peck on someone your own size.

Why did the frog buy a rod and reel?

He wanted to do some fly fishing.

What did the judge say when a skunk walked in?

Odor (Order) in the court!

How did the kangaroo convict escape?

He jumped bail.

Why did the pig go to the casino?

He wanted to play the slop machine.

What do you find in a pig mall?

Pork shops.

Why did the duck go ring! ring?

He got a phone bill.

How did the barber get rid of his unwanted rabbits?

He used hare remover.

How can you learn to speak to cows?

Take *moo*sic lessons.

Why did the elephant make a good reporter?

He had a great nose for news.

What owl has a band of merry men?

Robin *Hoot.*

What's big and white and scores a lot of strikes?

A bowler (polar) bear.

**What do you get if you cross a sheep
and a monkey?**

A bah-boon (baboon).

What lives in Washington, D.C. and eats fish?

The presidential seal.

Why didn't the nervous rooster cross the road?

He chickened out.

What's the hardest gift to buy for a giraffe?

A necktie.

**What do you get if you cross an elephant
and a skunk?**

I don't know, but you can smell it coming
from miles away.

FLAP!

FLAP!

FLAP!

FLAP!

What has four legs and flies?

A vul*chair* (vulture).

What kind of dog sniffs out new flowers?

A bud hound (bloodhound).

What did the duck do in the football game?

He made a first down.

What was Mrs. Chicken reading?

A yolk (joke) book.

What did the waiter say to the horse?

I can't take your order. That's not my stable.

What do moles like to eat?

Ground beef.

Why didn't the elephant get rich?

He was willing to work for peanuts.

Do you have to knock on Tarzan's front door?

No. Use the door buzzard (buzzer).

What game do mother hens play with their baby chicks?

Peck-a-boo.

What do you get if you cross a pile of dirt and a pig?

A groundhog.

Why couldn't the herd of deer buy lunch for everyone?

They only had one buck.

Where should you go if you lose your fish?

The lost-and-flounder department.

What reptile is really crumby?

The *cracker*dile.

What goes bounce! bounce! bounce! ouch?

A kangaroo accidentally hopping on a tack.

Where do cow artists put their works of art?

In a *moo*seum.

Why was the pony's hoof making a funny sound?

His horseshoe was a ringer.

**How can you tell the difference between
a zebra sergeant and a zebra private?**

The zebra sergeant has more stripes.

What do you call short stories written by hogs?

Pig tales.

Who is the funniest goat?

Billy the Kidder.

What do you call a minor bird accident?

A feather bender.

Why did the mole go to the store?

He heard they specialize in hole-sale (wholesale).

What does a squid wear on a cold day?

A coat of arms.

What has feathers and breaks into houses?

A robber ducky.

Where do horses stay in a hotel?

In the bridle suite.

What kind of buck carries a sample case?

A deer-to-deer (door-to-door) salesman.

What do you call a vaccination given to a boy deer?

Buck shot.

What dog do you find on a baseball field?

The catcher's mutt (mitt).

What did the beaver say to the tree?

It's been nice gnawing (knowing) you.

What calisthenic exercise do rabbits like to do?

Jumping jacks.

Who wiggles, hisses, and runs a country?

The president of the United Snakes.

What did Mr. Bird call his son?

A chirp off the old block.

What do elephants wear to the beach?

Bathing trunks.

**What do you get if you cross a dog
with a boomerang?**

A pooch that runs away but always comes back.

What is a rabbit's favorite song?

"Hoppy Birthday."

Why did the farmer name his pig Ink?

It kept running out of the pen.

What did the kitten say to the posse?

They went cat-away!

Why don't elephants take ballet lessons?

They look silly in tutus.

How do you drive a herd of cattle?

Use a *steer*ing wheel.

What bird lived in prehistoric times?

Crow-Magnon.

What kind of dog picks on smaller dogs?

A bully dog (bulldog).

GRRRR

What's soggy and has antlers?

A herd of raindeer (reindeer).

What do you call a well-dressed lion?

A dandy lion (dandelion).

Why did the sheep call the police?

It had been fleeced by a crook.

What do birds use to clean their nests?

Feather dusters.

Why do cats lick milk out of bowls?

They don't know how to use a straw.

What do skunks do when they get angry?

They raise a stink.

Which bird created a monster?

*Duck*tor Frankenstein.

Why wouldn't the leopard take a bath?

He didn't want to get spotlessly clean.

Why did the man wear a rabbit as a hat?

So no one would harm a hare on his head.

**How did the moose keep his antlers
from being stolen?**

He locked horns with another moose.

**What do you call a goat that lives
in the mountains?**

A hillbilly goat.

Why didn't the elephant tip the bellboy?

The boy wouldn't carry his trunk.

What squawks and jumps out of airplanes?

A parrot-trooper.

What is the skunk's motto?

Walk softly and carry a big stink.

What holiday do dogs like best?

Howl-a-ween.

What do you call a crazy chicken?

A cuckoo cluck.